The Story Of Yeshua
Whom The World Calls Jesus, The Christ

by Ken Small

©Copyright 2022 Ken Small

Let us follow truth wherever it leads.
Socrates

Distributed by
Excalibur Publishinging,
San Antonio, Texas

WordsOfWisdomByKen.com

INDEX

	Page
Chapter 1	3
The Beginning	
Chapter 2	5
Jesus' Birth and Boyhood	
Chapter 3	15
His Miracles	
Chaper 4	33
His Teachings	
Chapter 5	45
His Trial, Torture And Crucifixion	
Chapter 6	59
Jesus' Burial	
Chapter. 7	63
His Resurrection	
Chapter. 8	71
His Ascension	

Chapter 1
The Beginning

In the beginning was the Word, and the Word was with God, and the Word was God. He was in the world, and the world was made through Him, and the world did not know Him.

He came to His own, and His own did not receive Him. But as many as received Him, to them He gave the right to become children of God, to those who believe in His name. And the Word became flesh, and dwelt among us (John 1:1.10-12,14).

Chapter 2
Jesus' Birth and Boyhood

Now in the sixth month the angel Gabriel was sent by God to a city of Galilee, named Nazareth, to a virgin betrothed to a man whose name was Joseph, of the house of David. The virgin's name was Mary. The angel said to her, "Rejoice, highly favored one, the Lord is with you; blessed are you among women!" (Luke 1:26-28). "And behold, you will conceive in your womb and bring forth a Son, and shall call His name JESUS" (Luke 1:31).

Mary said to the angel, "How can this be, since I do not know a man?" And the angel answered and said to her, "The Holy Spirit will come upon you, and the power of the Highest will overshadow you; therefore, also, that Holy One who is to be born will be called the Son of God." Then Mary said, "Behold the maidservant of the Lord! Let it be to me according to your word." And the angel departed from her (Luke 1:34,38).

Now the birth of Jesus Christ was as follows: After His mother Mary was betrothed to Joseph, before they came together, she was found with child of the Holy Spirit. Then Joseph her husband, being a just man, and not wanting to make her a public example, was minded to put her away secretly. But while he thought about these things, behold, an angel of the Lord appeared to him in a dream, saying, "Joseph, son of David, do not be afraid to take to you Mary your wife, for that which is conceived in her is of the Holy Spirit. And she will bring forth a Son, and you shall call His name JESUS, for He will save His people from their sins" (Matthew 1:18-21).

So all this was done that it might be fulfilled which was spoken by the Lord through the prophet, saying: "Behold, the virgin shall be with child, and bear a son, and they shall call His name Immanuel," which is translated, "God with us" (verses 22,23). "For unto us a Child is born, unto us a Son is given: and the government shall be upon His shoulder: and His name shall be called Wonderful, Counsellor, The mighty God, The everlasting Father, The Prince of Peace" (Isaiah 9:6 [KJV]).

Mary was a teenager, alone, scared, and with a huge mission. Overwhelmed doesn't even begin to describe what lay before her. Pregnant without 'knowing a man' was a difficult situation to explain to her parents and soon to be husband. Hardly there's a woman alive who would have

responded to the angel who told her of her pregnancy as politely as she did: "I am the Lord's servant. May it be to me as you have said" (Luke 1:38). All she had was an angel to break the news to Joseph and that was only in a dream to him. Mary's family and friends in all probability scorned her and doubted her integrity and purity. She almost lost the man who loved her because of disbelief and shame.

It came to pass in those days that a decree went out from Caesar Augustus that all the world should be registered. So all went to be registered, everyone to his own city. Joseph also went up from Nazareth, into Judea, to the city of David, which is called Bethlehem to be registered with Mary, his betrothed wife, who was with child (Luke 2:1-5).

She brought forth her firstborn Son, and wrapped Him in swaddling cloths, and laid Him in a manger, because there was no room for them in the inn (Luke 2:7).

Now there were in the same country shepherds living out in the fields, keeping watch over their flock by night. And behold, an angel of the Lord stood before them, and the glory of the Lord shone around them, and they were greatly afraid. Then the angel said to them, "Do not be afraid, for behold, I bring you good tidings of great joy which will be to all people. For there is born to you this day in the city of David a Savior, who is Christ the Lord. And this will be the sign to you: You will find a Babe wrapped in swaddling cloths, lying in a manger." And suddenly there was with the angel a multitude of the heavenly host praising God and saying: "Glory to God in the highest, And on earth peace, goodwill toward men."

So it was, when the angels had gone away from them into heaven, that the shepherds said to one another, "Let us now go to Bethlehem and see this thing that has come to pass, which the Lord has made known to us." And they came with haste and found Mary and Joseph, and the Babe lying in a manger (Luke 2:8-16).

Now when they had seen Him, they made widely known the saying which was told them concerning this Child. And all those who heard it marveled at those things which were told them by the shepherds (Luke 2:8-18).

Now after Jesus was born in Bethlehem of Judea in the days of Herod the king, behold, wise men from the East came to Jerusalem, saying, "Where is He who has been born King of the Jews? For we have seen His star in the East and have come to worship Him."

When they had come into the house, they saw the young Child with Mary His mother, and fell down and worshiped Him. And when they had opened their treasures they presented gifts to Him: gold, frankincense, and myrrh (Matthew 2:1,11). The wise men were wise not only because they sought the Christ-child, but that they brought Him something: **Gold** for his journey and sustenance while in Egypt, **Frankincense**, to keep Him from disease as He was born in a cave full of animals. It was also used to anoint offerings (Leviticus 2:1) and **Myrrh**, the first oil mentioned in the Old Testament (Genesis 37:25) and the last to be mentioned in the New Testament (Revelation 18:13), an antifungal, anti- inflammatory, antiseptic and anticatarrhal oil.

His parents went to Jerusalem every year at the Feast of the Passover. And when He was twelve years old, they went up to Jerusalem according to the custom of the feast. When they had finished the days, as they returned, the Boy Jesus lingered behind in Jerusalem. And Joseph and His mother did not know it; but supposing Him to have been in the company,

they went a day's journey, and sought Him among their relatives and acquaintances. So when they did not find Him, they returned to Jerusalem, seeking Him. After three days they found Him in the temple, sitting in the midst of the teachers, both listening to them and asking them questions. And all who heard Him were astonished at His understanding and answers. So when they saw Him, they were amazed; and His mother said to Him, "Son, why have You done this to us? Look, Your father and I have sought You anxiously." And He said to them, "Why did you seek Me? Did you not know that I must be about My Father's business?" (Luke 2:41-49).

He went down with them, and came to Nazareth, and was subject unto them, but His mother kept all these things in her heart. And Jesus increased in wisdom and stature (Luke 2: 51,52).

Jesus was close to His mother. When He was suffering excruciating pain while impaled upon the cross, He refused to die until He was assured that Mary, His mother, was properly taken care of after He would be gone (John 19:25-30).

Jesus, being filled with the Holy Spirit, returned from the Jordan and was led by the Spirit into the wilderness, being tempted for forty days by the devil. All that time He ate nothing and became very hungry.

Then the devil taking Him up on a high mountain, showed Him all the kingdoms of the world in a moment of time. And the devil said to Him, "All this authority I will give You, and their glory; for this has been delivered to me, and I give it to whomever I wish. Therefore, if you will worship before me, all will be Yours." And Jesus answered and said to him, "Get behind Me, Satan! For it is written, 'You shall worship the Lord your God, and Him only you shall serve.'

Now when the devil had ended every temptation, he departed from Him until an opportune time. Then Jesus returned in the power of the Spirit to Galilee, and news of Him went out through all the surrounding region. And He taught in their synagogues, being glorified by all (Luke 4:1,2,5-8,13-15).

Chapter 3
His Miracles

So it was, as the multitude pressed about Him to hear the word of God, that He stood by the Lake of Gennesaret, and saw two boats standing by the lake; but the fishermen had gone from them and were washing their nets. Then He got into one of the boats, which was Simon's, and asked him to put out a little from the land. And He sat down and taught the multitudes from the boat. When He had stopped speaking, He said to Simon, "Launch out into the deep and let down your nets for a catch." But Simon answered and said to Him, "Master, we have toiled all night and caught nothing; nevertheless at Your word I will let down the net." And when they had done this, they caught a great number of fish, and their net was breaking. So they signaled to their partners in the other boat to come and help them. And they came and filled both the boats, so that they began to sink.

When Simon Peter saw it, he fell down at Jesus' knees, saying, "Depart from me, for I am a sinful man, O Lord!" For he and all who were with him were astonished at the catch of fish which they had taken; and so also were James and John, the sons of Zebedee, who were partners with Simon. And Jesus said to Simon, "Do not be afraid. From now on you will catch men." So when they had brought their boats to land, they forsook all and followed Him (Luke 5:1-11).

There was a wedding in Cana of Galilee, and the mother of Jesus was there. Now both Jesus and His disciples were invited to the wedding. And when they ran out of wine, the mother of Jesus said to Him, "They have no wine." His mother said to the servants, "Whatever He says to you, do it." Now there were set there six waterpots of stone containing twenty or thirty gallons apiece. Jesus said to them, "Fill the waterpots with water." And they filled them up to the brim. And He said to them, "Draw some out now, and take it to the master of the feast." And they took it.

When the master of the feast had tasted the water that was made wine, and did not know where it came from (but the servants who had drawn the water knew), the master of the feast called the bridegroom. And he said to him, "Every man at the beginning sets out the good wine, and when the guests have well drunk, then the inferior. You have kept the good wine until now!" This beginning of signs Jesus did in Cana of Galilee, and manifested His glory; and His disciples believed in Him (John 2:1-3,5-11).

And it happened when He was in a certain city, that behold, a man who was full of leprosy saw Jesus; and he fell on his face and implored Him, saying, "Lord, if You are willing, You can make me clean." Then He put out His hand and touched him, saying, "I am willing; be cleansed." Immediately the leprosy left him. And He charged him to tell no one. However, the report went around concerning Him all the more; and great multitudes came together to hear, and to be healed by Him of their infirmities (Luke 5:12-15).

Now it happened on a certain day, as He was teaching, that there were Pharisees and teachers of the law sitting by, who had come out of every town of Galilee, Judea, and Jerusalem. And the power of the Lord was present to heal them. Then behold, men brought on a bed a man who was paralyzed, whom they sought to bring in and lay before Him. And when they could not find how they might bring him in, because of the crowd, they went up on the housetop and let him down with his bed through the tiling into the midst before Jesus. When He saw their faith He said to him, "Man, your sins are forgiven you." And the scribes and the Pharisees began to reason, saying, "Who is this who speaks blasphemies? Who can forgive sins but God alone?" But when Jesus perceived their thoughts, He answered and said to them, "Why are you reasoning in your hearts? Which is easier to say, 'Your sins are forgiven you,' or to say, 'Rise up and walk'? But that you may know that the Son of Man has power on earth to forgive sins." —He said to the  man who was paralyzed, "I say to you, arise, take up your bed, and go to your house." Immediately he rose up before them, took up what he had been lying on, and departed to his own house, glorifying God. And they were all amazed, and they glorified God and were filled with fear, saying, "We have seen strange things today" (Luke 5:17-26).

Now when Jesus had entered Capernaum, a centurion came to Him, pleading with Him, saying, "Lord, my servant is lying at home paralyzed, dreadfully tormented." And Jesus said to him, "I will come and heal him." The centurion answered and said, "Lord, I am not worthy that You should come under my roof. But only speak a word, and my servant will be healed." When Jesus heard it, He marveled, and said to those who followed, "Assuredly, I say to you, I have not found such great faith, not even in Israel!" Then Jesus said to the centurion, "Go your way; and as you have believed, so let it be done for you." And his servant was healed that same hour (Matthew 8:5-8,10,13).

When Jesus returned the multitude welcomed Him, for they were all waiting for Him. And behold, there came a man named Jairus, and he was a ruler of the synagogue. And he fell down at Jesus' feet and begged Him to come to his house, for he had an only daughter about twelve years of age, and she was dying. But as He went, the multitudes thronged Him.

Now a woman, having a flow of blood for twelve years, who had spent all her livelihood on physicians and could not be healed by any, came from behind and touched the border of His garment. And immediately her flow of blood stopped. And Jesus said, "Who touched Me?" When all denied it, Peter and those with him said, "Master, the multitudes throng and press You, and You say, "Who touched Me?" Now when the woman saw that she was not hidden, she came trembling; and falling down before Him, she declared to Him in the presence of all the people the reason she had touched Him and how she was healed immediately. And He said to her, "Daughter, be of good cheer; your faith has made you well. Go in peace" (Luke 8:40-45,47,48).

He went into a city called Nain; and many of His disciples went with Him, and a large crowd. And when He came near the gate of the city, behold, a dead man was being carried out, the only son of his mother; and she was a widow. And a large crowd from the city was with her. When the Lord saw her, He had compassion on her and said to her, "Do not weep." Then He came and touched the open coffin, and those who carried him stood still. And He said, "Young man, I say to you, arise." So he who was dead sat up and began to speak. And He presented him to his mother. Then fear came upon all, and they glorified God ... And this report about Him went throughout all Judea and all the surrounding region (Luke 7:11-17).

While He was still speaking, someone came from the ruler of the synagogue's house, saying to him, "Your daughter is dead. Do not trouble the Teacher."

But when Jesus heard it, He answered him, saying, "Do not be afraid; only believe, and she will be made well." When He came into the house All wept and mourned for her; but He said, "Do not weep; she is not dead, but sleeping." He put them all outside, took her by the hand and called, saying, "Little girl, arise." Then her spirit returned, and she arose immediately. And He commanded that she be given something to eat. And her parents were astonished. (Luke 8:49-52,54-56).

As He went out of Jericho with His disciples and a great multitude, blind Bartimaeus sat by the road begging. And when he heard that it was Jesus of Nazareth, he began to cry out and say, "Jesus, Son of David, have mercy on me!" So Jesus stood still and commanded him to be called. Then they called the blind man, saying to him, "Be of good cheer. Rise, He is calling you."

And throwing aside his garment, he rose and came to Jesus. So Jesus answered and said to him, "What do you want Me to do for you?" The blind man said to Him, "Rabboni, that I may receive my sight." Then Jesus said to him, "Go your way; your faith has made you well." And immediately he received his sight and followed Jesus on the road (Mark 10:46,47,49-52).

And when Jesus went out He saw a great multitude; and He was moved with compassion for them, and healed their sick. When it was evening, His disciples came to Him, saying, "This is a deserted place, and the hour is already late. Send the multitudes away, that they may go into the villages and buy themselves food." But Jesus said to them, "They do not need to go away. You give them something to eat."

And they said to Him, "We have here only five loaves and two fish." He said, "Bring them here to Me." Then he commanded the multitudes to sit down on the grass. And He took the five loaves and the two fish, and looking up to heaven, He blessed and broke and gave the loaves to the disciples; and the disciples gave to the multitudes. So they all ate and were filled, and they took up twelve baskets full of the fragments that remained. Now those who had eaten were about five thousand men, besides women and children (Matthew 14:14-21).

They sailed to the country of the Gadarenes, which is opposite Galilee. And when He stepped out on the land, there met Him a certain man from the city who had demons for a long time. And he wore no clothes, nor did he live in a house but in the tombs. When he saw Jesus, he cried out, fell down before Him, and with a loud voice said, "What have I to do with you, Jesus, Son of the Most High God? I beg You, do not torment me!

For He had commanded the unclean spirit to come out of the man. For it had often seized him, and he was kept under guard, bound with chains and shackles; and he broke the bonds and was driven by the demon into the wilderness.

Jesus asked him, saying, "What is your name?" And he said, "Legion," because many demons had entered him. And they begged Him that He would not command them to go out into the abyss (Luke 8:26-31).

Now a herd of many swine was feeding there on the mountain. So they begged Him that He would permit them to enter them. And He permitted them. Then the demons went out of the man and entered the swine, and the herd ran violently down the steep place into the lake and drowned.

When those who fed them saw what had happened, they fled and told it in the city and in the country. Then they went out to see what had happened, and came to Jesus, and found the man from whom the demons had departed, sitting at the feet of Jesus, clothed and in his right mind. And they were afraid.

Then the whole multitude of the surrounding region of the Gadarenes asked Him to depart from them, for they were seized with great fear. And He got into the boat and returned (Luke 8:32-35,37).

Now it happened, on a certain day, that He got into a boat with His disciples. And He said to them, "Let us cross over to the other side of the lake." And they launched out. But as they sailed He fell asleep. And a windstorm came down on the lake, and they were filling with water, and were in jeopardy.

And they came to Him and awoke Him, saying, "Master, Master, we are perishing!" Then He arose and rebuked the wind and the raging of the water. And they ceased, and there was a calm. But He said to them, "Where is your faith?" And they were afraid, and marveled, saying to one another, "Who can this be? For He commands even the winds and water, and they obey Him!" (Luke 8:22-25).

Immediately Jesus made His disciples get into the boat and go before Him to the other side. And when He had sent the multitudes away, He went up on the mountain by Himself to pray. Now when evening came, He was alone there. But the boat was now in the middle of the sea, tossed by the waves, for the wind was contrary. Now in the fourth watch of the night Jesus went to them, walking on the sea. And when the disciples saw Him walking on the sea, they were troubled, saying, "It is a ghost!" And they cried out for fear. But immediately Jesus spoke to them, saying, "Be of good cheer! It is I; do not be afraid." And Peter answered Him and said, "Lord, if it is You, command me to come to You on the water." So He said, "Come." And when Peter had come down out of the boat, he walked on the water to go to Jesus. But when he saw that the wind was boisterous, he was afraid; and beginning to sink he cried out, saying, "Lord, save me!" And immediately Jesus stretched out His hand and caught him, and said to him, "O you of little faith, why did you doubt" (Matthew 14:22-31).

Therefore I say to you, do not worry about your life, what you will eat or what you will drink; nor about your body, what you will put on. Is not life more than food and the body more than clothing? Look at the birds of the air, for they neither sow nor reap nor gather into barns; yet your heavenly Father feeds them. Are you not more value than they? (Matthew 6:25,26).

"Are not five sparrows sold for two copper coins? And not one of them is forgotten before God. But the very hairs of our head are all numbered. Do not fear therefore; you are of more value than many sparrows" (Matthew 10:29-31; Luke 12:6,7).

The little children were brought to Him that He might put His hands on them and pray, but the disciples rebuked them. But Jesus said, "Let the little children come to Me, and do not forbid them; for of such is the kingdom of heaven" (Matthew 19:13,14).

"Assuredly, I say to you, whoever does not receive the kingdom of God as a little child will by no means enter it" (Mark 10:15).

~~~~~~~~~~~~~~~

"And there are also many other things that Jesus did, which if they were written one by one, I suppose that even the world itself could not contain the books that would be written. Amen" (John 21:25).

Chapter 4
His Teachings

Seeing the multitudes, He went up on a mountain, and when He was seated His disciples came to Him. Then He opened His mouth and taught them, saying (Matthew 5:1).

"Blessed are you poor, for yours is the kingdom of God. Blessed are you who hunger now, for you shall be filled. Blessed are you who weep now, for you shall laugh. Blessed are you when men hate you, and when they exclude you ... and cast out your name as evil, for the Son of Man's sake. Rejoice in that day and leap for joy! For indeed your reward is great in heaven, for in like manner their fathers did to the prophets" (Luke 6:20-23).

"And just as you want men to do to you, you also do to them likewise love your enemies, do good, and lend, hoping for nothing in return; and your reward will be great, and you will be sons of the Most High. Therefore be merciful, just as your Father also is merciful" (Luke 6:31, 35,36).

"Judge not, and you shall not be judged. Condemn not, and you shall not be condemned. Forgive, and you will be forgiven. Give, and it will be given to you: good measure, pressed down, shaken together, and running over will be put into your bosom. For with the same measure that you use, it will be measured back to you" (Luke 6:37,38).

Now it happened as they went that He entered a certain village; and a certain woman named Martha welcomed Him into her house. And she had a sister called Mary, who also sat at Jesus' feet and heard His word.

But Martha was distracted with much serving, and she approached Him and said, "Lord, do You not care that my sister has left me to serve alone? Therefore tell her to help me." And Jesus answered and said to her, "Martha, Martha, you are worried and troubled about many things. But one thing is needed, and Mary has chosen that good part, which will not be taken away from her" (Luke 10:38-42).

He said to them in His teaching, "Beware of the scribes, who desire to go around in long robes, love greetings in the marketplaces, the best seats in the synagogues, and the best places at feasts, who devour widows' houses, and for a pretense make long prayers. These will receive greater condemnation" (Mark 12:38-40).

Now Jesus sat opposite the treasury and saw how the people put money into the treasury. And many who were rich put in much. Then one poor widow came and threw in two mites. So He called His disciples to Himself and said to them, "Assuredly, I say to you that this poor widow has put in more than all those who have given to the treasury; for they all put in out of their abundance, but she out of her poverty put in all that she had, her whole livelihood" (Mark 12:41-44).

So He came to a city of Samaria. Now Jacob's well was there. Jesus therefore, being wearied from His journey, sat thus by the well. A woman of Samaria came to draw water. Jesus said to her. "Give Me a drink." Then the woman of Samaria said to Him, "How is it that You, being a Jew, ask a drink from me, a Samaritan woman?" For Jews have no dealings with Samaritans. Jesus answered and said to her, "If you knew the gift of God, and who it is who says to you, 'Give Me a drink,' you would have asked Him, and He would have given you living water" (John 4:5-10).

"The hour is coming, and now is, when the true worshipers will worship the Father in spirit and truth; for the Father is seeking such to worship Him. God is Spirit, and those who worship Him must worship in spirit and truth" (John 4:23-24).

One of the Pharisees asked Him to eat with him. And He went to the Pharisees's house, and sat down to eat. Behold a woman in the city who was a sinner brought an alabaster flask of fragrant oil, and stood at His feet behind Him weeping; and she began to wash His feet with her tears, and wiped them with the hair of her head; and she kissed His feet and anointed them with the fragrant oil. Now when the Pharisee saw this, he spoke to himself, saying, "This Man, if He were a prophet, would know who and what manner of woman this is who is touching Him, for she is a sinner." And Jesus answered and said to him, "Simon, I have  something to say to you. There was a certain creditor who had two debtors. One owed five hundred denarii, and the other fifty. And when they had nothing with which to repay, he freely forgave them both. Tell Me, therefore, which of them will love him more?" Simon answered and said, "I suppose the one whom he forgave more."

And He said to him, "You have rightly judged." Then He turned to the woman and said to Simon, "Do you see this woman? I entered your house; you gave Me no water for My feet, but she has washed my feet with her tears and wiped them with the hair of her head. You gave Me no kiss, but this woman has not ceased to kiss My feet since the time I came in. You did not anoint My head with oil, but this woman has anointed My feet with fragrant oil. Therefore I say to you, her sins, which are many, are forgiven, for she loved much. But to whom little is forgiven, the same loves little" (Luke 7:36-47).

Philip said to Him, "Lord, show us the Father, and it is sufficient for us." Jesus said to him, "Have I been with you so long, and yet you have not known Me, Phillip? He who has seen Me has seen the Father" (John 14:8,9). "I and My Father are one" (John 10:30). "Therefore I said to you ... if you do not believe that I am He, you will die in your sins" (John 8:24). Then one of the scribes came and ... asked Him, "Which is the first commandment of all?"

Jesus answered him, "The first of all the commandments is: Hear, O Israel, the Lord our God, the Lord is one. And you shall love the Lord your God with all your heart, with all your soul, with all your mind, and with all your strength. This is the first commandment. And the second, like it, is this: You shall love your neighbor as yourself. There is no other commandment greater than these" (Mark 12:28-31).

They brought little children to Him, that He might touch them; but the disciples rebuked those who brought them. But when Jesus saw it, He was greatly displeased and said to them, "Let the little children come to Me, and do not forbid them; for of such is the kingdom of God. Assuredly, I say to you, whoever does not receive the kingdom of God as a little child will by no means enter it." And He took them up in His arms, laid His hands on them, and blessed them (Mark 10:13-16).

Now early in the morning He came again into the temple, and all the people came to Him; and He sat down and taught them. Then the scribes and Pharisees brought to Him a woman caught in adultery. And when they had set her in the midst, they said to Him, "Teacher, this woman was caught in adultery, in the very act. Now Moses, in the law, commanded us that such should be stoned. But what do You say?" This they said, testing Him, that they might have something of which to accuse Him. But Jesus stooped down and wrote on the ground with His finger, as though he did not hear.

So when they continued asking Him, He raised Himself up and said to them, "He who is without sin among you, let him throw a stone at her first." Then those who heard it, being convicted by their conscience, went out one by one. And Jesus was left alone, and the woman standing in the midst. He said to her, "Woman, where are those accusers of yours? Has no one condemned you?" She said, "No one, Lord." And Jesus said to her, "Neither do I condemn you; go and sin no more" (John 8:2-7,9-11).

Now as He sat on the Mount of Olives opposite the temple, Peter, James, John, and Andrew asked Him privately, "What will be the sign when all these things will be fulfilled?" And Jesus, answering them, began to say: "Take heed that no one deceives you. For many will come in My name, saying, 'I am He,' and will deceive many. But when you hear of wars and rumors of wars, do not be troubled; for such things must happen, but the end is not yet. For nation will rise against nation, and kingdom against kingdom. And there will be earthquakes in various places, and there will be famines and troubles. These are the beginning of sorrows."

But of that day and hour no one knows, not even the angels in heaven. Take heed, watch and pray; for you do not know when the time is.

It is like a man going to a far country, who left his house and gave authority to his servants, and to each his work, and commanded the doorkeeper to watch. Watch therefore, for you do not know when the master of the house is coming — in the evening, at midnight, at the crowing of the rooster, or in the morning — lest, coming suddenly, he find you sleeping. And what I say to you, I say to all: Watch" (Mark 13:3-8,32-37).

"When the Son of Man comes in His glory, and all the holy angels with Him, then He will sit on the throne of His glory. All the nations will be gathered before Him, and He will separate them one from another, as a shepherd divides his sheep from the goats. Then He will also say to those on the left hand, 'Depart from Me, you cursed, into the everlasting fire prepared for the devil and his angels: for I was hungry and you gave Me no food; I was thirsty and you gave Me no drink; I was a stranger and you did not take Me in, naked and you did not clothe Me, sick and in prison and you did not visit Me'" (Matthew 25:31,32,41-43).

Then they also will answer Him, saying, 'Lord, when did we see You hungry or thirsty or a stranger or naked or sick or in prison, and did not minister to You?'

Then He will answer them, saying, 'Assuredly, I say to you, inasmuch as you did not do it to one of the least of these, you did not do it to Me.' And these will go away into everlasting punishment, but the righteous into eternal life (Matthew 25:44-46).

Chapter 5
Trial, Torture, and Crucifixion

When morning came, all the chief priests and elders of the people plotted against Jesus to put Him to death. And when they had bound Him, they led Him away and delivered Him to Pontius Pilate the governor. While he was sitting on the judgment seat, his wife sent to him, saying, "Have nothing to do with that just Man, for I have suffered many things today in a dream because of Him." Pilate said to them, "What then shall I do with Jesus who is called Christ?" They all said to him, "Let Him be crucified!" Then the governor said, "Why, what evil has He done?" But they cried out all the more, saying, "Let Him be crucified!"

When Pilate saw that he could not prevail at all, but rather that a tumult was rising, he took water and washed his hands before the multitude, saying, "I am innocent of the blood of this just Person. You see to it" (Matthew 27:1,2,19,22-24).

So then Pilate took Jesus and scourged Him (John 19:1).

No Greater Love

"Without shedding of blood there is no remission [of sin] (Hebrews 9:22)."

The soldier took Jesus into the Praetorium and gathered the whole garrison around Him. Yeshua's hands were chained to a post in the middle of the courtyard. The Roman soldiers stripped Him of His clothes and started the brutal process of 'scourging.' First, they proceeded to beat His face with their fists, then pulled out His beard with their hands. Rods were used to slash His body, tearing into the flesh and causing blood to flow. A twisted a crown of thorns and shoved on His head. It's thorn had one to six-inch spikes, causing the blood to flow freely into the Messiah's eyes. Then they started striking His face and head with a reed and spitting on Him.

A leather flagellum (a whip with several leather thongs) had pieces of iron and sharp sheep bones attached to each of its ends. As the sharp metal and bones on the whip tore away the Messiah's flesh, muscles were sliced open and the arteries torn, spurting blood. Most victims died from the torture. Isaiah had prophesied, "His visage (face) was marred more than any man. And His form (body) more than the sons of men" (Isaiah 52:14).

Thirty-nine times the diabolical flagellum tore apart the Savior's body. When they were through mocking Yeshua, they led Him away to be crucified (Matthew 27:27,29-31).

As hideous as the torture was, there was a divine purpose for the beating. In addition to suffering and dying for the redemption of sins that was to all mankind, Yeshua was also being wounded for our healing, for: "By whose stripes you were healed" (1 Peter 2:24).

And a great multitude of the people followed Him, and women who also mourned and lamented Him (Luke 23:27).

The intensity of Christ's suffering even before His actual crucifixion is revealed by the fact that after a night of torture He was too weak to carry His own cross the 650 yards to the place of execution. It was therefore placed upon Simon of Cyrenian (Luke 23:26).

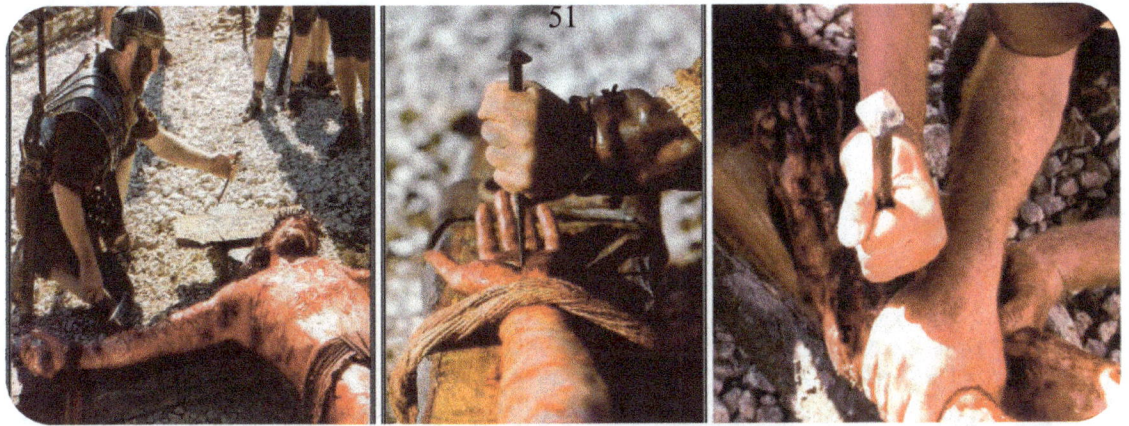

Yeshua's flesh hung in ribbons. The splinters tore into His exposed back and shoulders causing still more blood and increased pain. A few of His bones were exposed from the flagellum's fury. By now, Yeshua was already dehydrated. The miracle was that He was still living. *And when they had come to the place called Calvary, there they crucified Him, and the criminals, one on the right hand and the other on the left* (Luke 23:33).

And the people stood looking on ... Now there stood by the cross of Jesus, Mary Magdalene (Luke 23:35, John 19:25).

Arriving at Golgotha, the soldiers flung Yeshua to the ground and stretched His arms upon the crossbar for size. The executioner took a square spike, about a third of an inch think, and drove it with a single blow between the carpal, or wrist bones, (not through Yeshua's palm, as the weight of His body would have ripped through the flesh of His hands). In Roman times, the wrists were considered to be part of the hand — which explains the various Scriptures referring to the 'nail prints in His hands.'

Then one of the criminals who were hanged blasphemed Him, saying, "If You are the Christ, save Yourself and us." But the other, answering, rebuked him, saying, "Do you not even fear God, seeing you are under the same condemnation? And we indeed justly, for we receive the due reward of our deeds; but this Man has done nothing wrong." Then he said to Jesus, "Lord, remember me when You come into Your kingdom." And Jesus said to him, "Assuredly, I say to you, today you will be with Me in Paradise" (Luke 23:39-43).

The flaming pain caused by the spikes through the median nerves in Yeshua wrists exploded up His arms, into His brain, and down His spine. The spike was burning through the nerves between the metatarsal bones of His feet jerked His body erect. Then the leg muscles convulsed driving Yeshua's body downward. Over and over this process continued.

According to Mark's Gospel, Yeshua (Jesus) endured the torment of crucifixion for some six hours from the third hour, at approximately 9 am, until His death at the ninth hour, corresponding to about 3 pm. Exhaustion, shock, dehydration, and paralysis were draining Jesus' endurance as His blood coagulated and separated into serum and clotted cells — dying one at a time.

The angels in heaven looked on in horror, and awaited Yeshua to give the order to attack; but the order never came. In His love for mankind, He held back the fatal command; "For while we were yet sinners, Christ died for us" (Romans 5:8). And instead of the decree to exterminate those tormentors who so sadistically were killing Him, Yeshua cried: "Father forgive them, for they do not know what they do" (Luke 23:34). And so, we who deserved death, received the promise of life.

Jesus said, "It is finished!" And bowing His head, He gave up His spirit (John19:30). Now it was about the sixth hour, and there was darkness over all the earth until the ninth hour. Then the sun was darkened, and the veil of the temple was torn in two (Luke 23:44,45).

And Jesus cried out with a loud voice, and breathed His last. Then the veil of the temple was torn in two from top to bottom. So when the centurion, who stood opposite Him, saw that He cried out like this and breathed His last, he said "Truly this Man was the Son of God" (Mark:37-40).

Because it was the Preparation *Day*, that the bodies should not remain on the cross on the Sabbath (for that Sabbath was a high day), the Jews asked Pilate that their legs might be broken, and that they might be taken away. Then the soldiers came and broke the legs of the first and of the other who was crucified with Him. But when they came to Jesus and saw that He was already dead, they did not break His legs. But one of the soldiers pierced His side with a spear, and immediately blood and water came out (John 19:31-34).

Earlier, solders used a spear to give Jesus a sponge mixed with wine and myrrh to ease His pain. He refused it. Later, they used a spear to pierce Jesus side to make sure He was dead (Mark 15:23). For these things were done that the Scripture should be fulfilled, "Not one of His bones shall be broken." And again another Scripture says, "They shall look on Him whom they pierced" (John 19:36,37).

Now behold, there was a man named Joseph, a council member, a good and just man. This man went to Pilate and asked for the body of Jesus. Then he took it down." (Luke 23:50,52,53).

Chapter 6
Jesus' Burial

He (Joseph) wrapped it (the body of Jesus) in a clean linen cloth, and laid it in his new tomb which he had hewn out of the rock; and he rolled a large stone against the door of the tomb, and departed (Matthew 27:59,60). And the women who had come with Him from Galilee followed after, and they observed the tomb and how His body was laid. Then they returned and prepared spices and fragrant oils. And they rested on the Sabbath according to the commandment (Luke 23:55,56).

On the next day, which followed the Day of Preparation, the chief priests and Pharisees gathered together to Pilate, saying, "Sir, we remember, while He was still alive, how that deceiver said, 'After three days I will rise.' Therefore command that the tomb be made secure until the third day, lest His disciples come by night and steal Him away, and say to the people, He has risen from the dead." Pilate said to them, "You have a guard; go your way, make it as secure as you know how." So they went and made the tomb secure, sealing the stone and setting the guard (Matthew 27:62-66).

Chapter 7

His Resurrection

Now after the Sabbath, as the first day of the week began to dawn, Mary Magdalene and the other Mary came to see the tomb. And behold, there was a great earthquake; for an angel of the Lord descended from heaven, and came and rolled back the stone from the door, and sat on it. His countenance was like lightning and his clothing as white as snow. And the guards shook for fear of him, and became like dead men (Matthew 28:1-4).

The angel answered and said to the women, "Do not be afraid, for I know that you seek Jesus who was crucified. He is not here; for He is risen, as He said. Come, see the place where the Lord lay. And go quickly and tell His disciples that He is risen from the dead ..." (Matthew 28:5-7).

She ran and came to Simon Peter, and to the other disciple, whom Jesus loved, and said to them, "They have taken away the Lord out of the tomb, and we do not know where they have laid Him" (John 20:2,3). But Peter arose and ran to the tomb; and stooping down, he saw the linen cloths lying by themselves; and he departed marveling to himself at what had happened (Luke 24:12).

But Mary stood outside by the tomb weeping ... she turned around and saw Jesus standing there, and did not know that it was Jesus. Jesus said to her, "Woman, why are you weeping? Whom are you seeking?" She, supposing Him to be the gardener, said to Him, "Sir, if You have carried Him away, tell me where You have laid Him, and I will take Him away" (John 20:11,14,15).

Jesus said to her, "Mary!" She said to Him, "Rabboni!" (which is to say, Teacher). Jesus saith unto her, "Do not cling to Me." (John 20: 16,17).

Mary Magdalene came and told the disciples that she had seen the Lord and that He had spoken these things to her (John 20:18). And when they heard that he was alive and had been seen by her, they did not believe (Mark 16:11).

If you look at the original Greek form this commandment recorded in John 20:17 — Μή μου ἅπτου (*Me mou aptou*), uses the imperative mood of the verb (*h*)*aptein,"to fasten"* — more accurately: *"Do not cling to Me"* or *'Do not detain Me now."*

Then, the same day at evening, being the first day of the week, when the doors were shut where the disciples were assembled, for fear of the Jews, Jesus came and stood in the midst, and said to them, "Peace be with you." When He had said this, He showed them His hands and His side. Then the disciples were glad when they saw the Lord.

Now Thomas, called the Twin, one of the twelve, was not with them when Jesus came. The other disciples therefore said to him, "We have seen the Lord." So he said to them, "Unless I see in His hands the print of the nails, and put my finger into the print of the nails, and put my hand into His side, I will not believe" (John 20:19,20,24,25).

And after eight days His disciples were again inside, and Thomas with them. Jesus came, the doors being shut, and stood in the midst, and said, "Peace to you!" Then He said to Thomas, "Reach your finger here, and look at My hands; and reach your hand here, and put it into My side. Do not be unbelieving, but believing."

And Thomas answered and said to Him, "My Lord and my God!" Jesus said to him, "Thomas, because you have seen Me, you have believed. Blessed are those who have not seen and yet have believed" (John 20:26-29).

Chapter
Jesus' Ascension

He led them out as far as Bethany, and He lifted up His hands and blessed them. Now it came to pass, while He blessed them, that He was parted from them and carried up into heaven (Luke 24:50-51).

And while they looked steadfastly toward heaven as He went up, behold, two men stood by them in white apparel, who also said, "Men of Galilee, why do you stand gazing up into heaven? This same Jesus, who was taken up from you into heaven, will so come in like manner as you saw Him go into heaven" (Acts 1:10,11).

And they worshiped Him, and returned to Jerusalem with great joy (Luke 24:52).

The Way To Heaven Is Simple

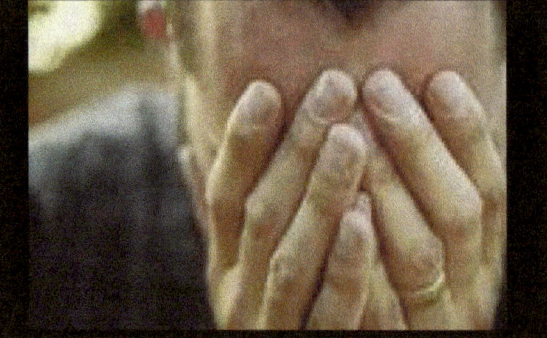

Tell Yeshua that you're sorry for all the bad things you've done[1]

Be baptized in Yeshua's name so that your sins will be washed away[2]

Open your heart and let Yeshua fill you with His Spirit[3]

Know and declare that Yeshua is God[4]

[1] Romans 3:23; 1 John 1:8,9; Luke 13;5: Acts 2:38
[2] Mark 16:16; Acts 2:38; 8:16; 10:48; 19:5; 22:16; Colossians 3:17
[3] Ezekiel 36:27; Romans 8:9; John 3:5; 4:24; Acts 1:5; 2:38
[4] *John 1:1,14; 8:24; 10:30; 12:45; 14:9; 1 Timothy 6:14-16*

Just 8 Simple Steps

Live a clean life "without which no one shall see God"[2]

Use the gifts and talents that God has given to you[1]

Love God with all your heart, soul, mind, and strength[3]

Going Home[4]

[1] 1 Timothy 4:14; 2 Timothy 1:6; 1 Corinthians 7:7
[2] Leviticus 20:7,8; Hebrews 12:14; 2 Corinthians 7:1
[3] Joshua 22:5; Jeremiah 29:13; Mark 12:30; John 14:115
[4] *1 Thessalonians 4:16,17; 1 Corinthians 15:51-53; Matthew 24:37-44*

*Since Jesus is the light of the world,
isn't it time to run into the sunshine?
He is the answer you been searching for.
Why are you waiting?
You've waited long enough!*

Soon after Yeshua (Jesus) ascended into Heaven, the Jews started stoning Christians to death. During the Dark Ages, Catholics first tortured, then burned alive millions who believed in Jesus. Hitler, Stalin, and Mao imprisoned, tortured, and starved in concentration camps, Christians throughout Germany, Russia, and China. Muslem terrorists slaughter believers by the thousands; while those in the occult try to cast spells upon them; but **Christianity** flourishes. Why? Because it **is not a religion — it's the relationship** between God and His people.

Soon Jesus will take His children to a place that is beyond comprehension in wonder and beauty. "... Eye hath not seen, nor ear heard, neither have entered into the heart of man, the things which God hath prepared for those that love him" (1 Corinthians 2:9). You will be sprung from the confines of time and space to be what you were originally created to be. Heaven is a place where limitations no longer exist — endless possibilities are all waiting to be explored and enjoyed. Imagine complete and total freedom: riding upon the wings of the winds, running with lions, or sliding down waterfalls. Close your eyes and remember your sweetest success or most cherished and loving moment. Heaven dwarfs all these as the mighty ocean dwarfs the tiny rain drop. Words are too inadequate to describe the endless possibilities and pleasures that await.

To ensure that you enjoy all this and more, you will have a perfectly developed body that will never tire, become sick, or grow old — one that is immortal (1 Corinthians 15:51-54). "And God shall wipe away all tears from their eyes; there shall be no more death, neither sorrow, nor crying, neither shall there be any more pain" (Revelation 21:4). Here you can meet and talk with Yeshua (Jesus) face to face — and I assure you that He is grander, more beautiful, more compassionate, and more loving than one can imagine! Content and safe in His presence, you shall reign with Him forever (Revelation 22:5).

Since we all come from God (Jeremiah 1:5), going to Yeshua is going back home (Ecclesiastes 12:7).

> *I am the door. If anyone enters by Me, he will be saved ...*
>
> John 10:9

www.ingramcontent.com/pod-product-compliance
Lightning Source LLC
LaVergne TN
LVHW061253060426
835507LV00017B/2052